Zyanna Rosado

Dear Readers,

These poems were written at times where I felt dark and alone. I appreciate the opportunity to be able to share these works, with which I feel a deep passion for. I'd like to give a special thank you to my parents for instilling hard work into my brain, even though at times I didn't want to do it. Thank you for taking the time to walk through this part of my life with me; stay tuned for brighter times.

Table of Contents

1. To Whom It May Concern

2. Ignorance

3. You'll Be Ight

4. Intoxication

5. What's the Point

6. Lost Soul

7. Lay in It

8. Waves

9. Society

10. Victory

11. Conquered

12. Bleeding Out

13. Basket

14. Force

Zyanna Rosado   *Confessions of a Broken Soul*

To Whom it May Concern,

Please excuse my absent mindedness,

Understand my lack of kindness,

I've been sick.

Sick of these days where I've been stuck in a cloudy phase.

I'm begging to find this clarity,

My judgement has been mad at me,

In what way can it be put at ease?

I'm tired, I'm tired, I'm tired, I'm tired.

If you have any questions,

Please don't feel free to contact me.

My phone will not be next to me

I'm begging you just to let me be.

                                                                       Thank you,

                                                                       Zyanna Rosado

Ignorance

Stumbling using my laughter as tears

Trying to patch myself up, but you handed me shears.

Told me you couldn't do it, but I didn't hear,

Now being empty is one of my strongest fears.

You took me apart and you lay me down bare

I was trying to breathe but you blocked off my air

Yet, I suffocated you?

I held you up high,

And you climbed down with ease

And my arms broke holding you

My tear-filled eyes dried with the breeze.

I needed help from you.

I begged and I pleaded, you ignored me.

You couldn't even tell when my attitude was changing.

But I acted like neglect was alright.

I started being silent in order to not burden you with my struggles.

Zyanna Rosado — *Confessions of a Broken Soul*

I lost my sense of self because my head was stuck so far up your ass,

I forgot eventually you'd shit on me too.

I forgot eventually you'd want to breathe without me

So, you'd drain my lungs and forget to fill them back up

I forgot that in building you up,

I'd be too distracted to build up myself because I'd expect the action to be reciprocated.

I forgot that actions usually aren't reciprocated,

And expecting you to meet me halfway was a failure from the start.

You keep acting like a Nissan needing a push to start

You gassed me up, but you used regular.

burnt my engine because I am premium.

Didn't take care of my interior because you're the only one who saw it.

So, when I finally stopped being what you wanted

You replaced me with a newer model.

Made me feel as though I wasn't enough.

But really it was you.

Too insecure to be grateful for what you already have.

Too nonchalant to keep up with the maintenance required.

I'm sorry that I came with too much baggage for your liking.

Maybe you just needed a bit more experience.

I just needed to know somebody cared.

I just needed somewhere to release the pain, so I could stop hurting myself.

I just needed someone to understand what made me like this.

Instead of making me feel crazy every moment they get.

People say patience is a virtue,

I say patience requires faith.

And even if with you my patience wore thin,

I still pray for you.

I'll still think about you.

And I'll still be in pain.

I know I'm hurting.

I know my head is stuck

I know my heart is broken

I know I love you.

But I don't need you

Nor do I any man to give me reassurance to love myself

I know that I'm hurting,

But one day you'll hurt to.

You'll Be Ight

You're all alone,

you stand tall,

but no one's helping you up

because we live in a culture

that tells a man he must be stuck

walking around with a mask

he's not allowed to take off

because a man,

must be strong,

don't cry,

he must be tough.

if he gets lost

in his head

no one may see the changes

because growing up

he was told

that emotions are

for ladies

in relationships

he never learned

to express himself

so, he struggles

he fights

with his wife

begging

for something other

than a straight face

or anger

because those

were the only two feelings

he was "allowed" to display

he has to prove his masculinity,

he has to bring home the funds,

he has to be the rock for his family

he must show his kids that men don't cry

but this repeats a cycle

that he is not comfortable with breaking

and, thus, it continues.

which sends more

men into an abyss

of actions he is oblivious to.

so now he is depressed,

but he doesn't understand

this is a thing

so, he masks his sadness

and it boils down

to the idea

"I'll be ight."

Intoxication

Intoxication runs deep through my veins

And, no, I haven't drank

I haven't smoked

I haven't shot

but I feel pain

so intense

that my heart

feels like it stopped,

I am here

and I am now

but I was lost

in the crowd I

finally found

myself

and when I found

I fell out

did you cry

did you feel

when I went missing

did you try to heal

me?

Or did you just assume

that the problems were out of your hands?

did you question your ability to take a stand?

did you try as you might?

did you fight for my life?

because I lost it.

but I'm intoxicated so I can feel you.

and I know that even if you don't try

you're here

and I know

that at night

your mind wanders and

fights yourself

because of the things that you didn't do

to prove

you were worthy of my love

but I'll heal you

because that's what I do

I'll put you above my feelings

and take in your pain

your guilt

your anger

it'll be for me.

and I'll forget

for the time being

that I have problems too

because for now

it feels better

to take the ones from you.

What's the Point?

But tell me?

What is the point,

Of saying how you feel,

When no one seems to be listening?

Lost Soul

A lost soul torn between two souls

divided

did I just reiterate my situation?

maybe not directly without thinking

about the reciprocation

I try to make this imagination my home like some personification

but the attributes don't match with the complications

Divergence.

Diverging into this conversation

Uncertain.

Of where I'm at and what I'm contemplating

An ocean.

Of thoughts drifting toward the edge

Control me.

So, I don't leave anything unsaid.

Break me.

So, I can feel whole again

And if you use me,

Just make sure you do it until the end

Just don't confuse me.

Because I never meant what I said.

Lay in It

I walk a straight and narrow line in which only I can succumb to.

But lately it feels as though I've been pulled over by the police,

Who have asked me to take a sobriety test that I just cannot pass.

Not because I'm intoxicated,

But

It's simply that I seem to have forgotten how to walk alone.

And my legs went numb when I tried to stand on my own two feet.

My brain hasn't been sending messages fast enough to the rest of my body.

I think my nervous system has been pulled like string cheese.

But I'd like to understand who seems to have looked at my sanity as a snack.

Slowly, but, surely I am being drawn apart.

Quietly, I've lost my mind

but for some reason the voice in the back of my head got louder.

Constantly telling me to do things that I wish I could say no too.

But, my sheer will seems to have taken a long overdue trip

to a place with no reception.

I guess it needed a break from me.

Maybe I became too overpowering.

Or maybe there's a lack of commitment within myself.

You see, decisions have always been challenging to me.

My scale has recently been completely off balance.

As I've been trying to decipher the negatives and positives of my actions.

It's gotten to the point that the bad outweighs the good,

but I'm still trying to figure out which negative entity to let go of.

I've realized I'm full of flawless flaws.

I just had to accept that I've made my bed,

It's time to finally lay in it.

Waves

my sadness comes in waves.

one behind the other

crashing down.

at times I feel I've finally reached the middle.

and for some reason,

I can't seem to keep my feet grounded.

so, I'm engulfed under the wave,

and forced to stand tall, with a clean slate each time.

hopefully, I don't forget what I've learned,

because next time, I might drown.

Society

A society unheard of

Lost woods of the forgotten

Times where no one ever hurt us

counting everything they've gotten.

Sad eyes fill the pasture

But no one's ever seen them cry.

Those tears filled the rivers faster

The tears were derived from the sky.

Because God has given everything, he could

But no one ever seemed to listen

Confused and misunderstood

in those lost woods, connection was missing.

Compare my heart to those forgotten

You'll see one thing you never heard of

if you look deep in my soul, you'll see it's rotten

And honestly, you'll leave for sure, love.

Victory

Broken and torn, lost in the swarm

Of people around me promising to give me more

But they cannot.

Because most promises are empty,

Controlled within their minds

But less controlled when put into action

Is that a reason we're scared?

Is that that reason why our hearts are in despair?

While our heads are in the air,

And my

Eyes are blinded

Blind

I'm going through my life blind

Multiplying my negativity accidentally

Struggling with my mental

Zyanna Rosado

Confessions of a Broken Soul

Mentally

I'm stuck somewhere in my 30's.

Yearning for consistency

Hoping one day I'll see better

Then what's in front of me.

New paths to continue my endeavors

Because I can't seem to choose the right way to ruin my life.

Ruining time

Praying for a knife

To appear and slice through my obstacles

Running through my options now

Petrified by my reaction, I bow

At my creator

For making me great

Even though an instruction manual was forgotten

Will I ever have one?

Or will I be forced to do this alone?

Maybe one day I'll be happy.

Or maybe one day I'll be too distracted

To even notice I've been standing in hell's fire

For some reason it isn't as hot as I pictured it to be.

But I guess the pictures all I see

For now, maybe I'll just take this as a victory.

Conquered

Getting conquered

through my unconsciousness.

Convinced that civilization has no options

Misinterpretations through my fallacies,

Of a life I created with no majesty.

Because even though I should be in charge

I've reached paths to higher situations

Which I can say have been past the credits

and onto the preview to the next life I wished for.

Open policies to control my hopes and promises

I was unsure I'd ever reach the opportunity to fulfill

My destiny wasn't chosen for me it just fell.

Into my lap because I got stuck with a hell

I never meant to create

But now I'm living it further and further and I'm becoming irate

My future is becoming immaculate

Losing control of my emotions

I thought we hashed this shit

But I was lied to.

No more options to this situation

I was dying to

Live a new life without burning

But I can't help it with this world, we're learning.

Bleeding Out

This God forsaken, everlasting love

To which I call my own.

I call on you to count the ways in which I bleed

From which veins I am draining out of.

Misery is pain, and pain is ease.

But no one said either were easy.

The commas were placed ever so slightly on my heart.

My mind came equipped with a toe-tag.

I felt as though I had diamonds in my eyes,

yet you treated me like I was topaz.

Risen above the hatred and envy,

was anger revealing itself.

My head feels excessively neglected these days.

I've been pondering reasons to live without you.

And among that my thoughts went completely black.

Instead I just look for reasons to avoid you.

Lacking in knowledge I'd examined this terrain falsely.

Tomorrow night I'll beg for an open gesture.

And once you give it, I'll take it on a limb.

Due to my being I'll forgive you,

And for the millionth time in our life,

you'll leave me bleeding out.

Basket

Remember when Mama said

not to put all your eggs in one basket?

Look at you now,

Falling so deep for a person who never planned to love you back.

You lost yourself, and you're hurting,

So, what will you do now?

Put yourself first, my love, or nobody will.

Force

I'll say this once, and once only.

You cannot make a man love you when he doesn't.

You cannot force your love upon him,

Otherwise it will draw him further away.

Stop wasting your energy on someone

God never sent for you.

Protect your heart at all costs

Because you're the only one who cares.

Made in the USA
Middletown, DE
13 September 2022